Charlie's "Be Kind" Day

WRITTEN BY PATRICIA SHELY MAHANY

ILLUSTRATED BY CINDY WASCO

Published by Standard Publishing, Cincinnati, Ohio
www.standardpub.com

ISBN 978-0-7847-1689-2

11 10 09   9 8 7 6 5 4 3

Standard®
P U B L I S H I N G
Bringing The Word to Life

Cincinnati, Ohio

Charlie woke up feeling grouchy.

He jumped out of bed.

He stepped on Jeremy's truck.

"Ouch!" Charlie yelled.

"Jeremy, I don't like you!"

Jeremy threw his pillow at Charlie.

He yelled, "I don't need a big brother!

Get out of my room."

Mother heard the awful noise.

Mother called,

"Charlie, come eat your breakfast."

"Mom," Charlie said, "Jeremy makes me mad.

He never picks up his toys.

He says *my* room is *his* room.

I don't like him."

"Charlie, listen to some important words from God's Book.

'Be kind to one another,'" Mother read.

"You and Jeremy need to be kind to each other.

You are the oldest.

You can help Jeremy be kind.

Let's call today Charlie's 'Be Kind' day."

Charlie went to his room.

He thought about what Mother said.

It would be very hard to be kind all day.

But he would give it a try.

"Charlie," said Mother,

"Mrs. Rucker lost her kitten.

Will you go help her find Nicholas?"

Mrs. Rucker lived in the house next door.

Charlie heard a soft "Meow! Meow!"

"Nicholas, where are you?" he called.

Charlie went over to the garbage can.

"Nicholas!" Charlie laughed.

"How did you get in there?"

Nicholas was safe.

Mrs. Rucker was very happy.

She gave Charlie two quarters.

"Thank you for being a kind boy,"

Mrs. Rucker said.

Charlie knew what he would do
with the two quarters.
He wanted a new mini car.
Charlie hurried home.

Charlie wanted to play outside.
Mother said, "Jeremy has a cold.
He can't go out to play.
You'll have to play alone."

Charlie sat down in his wagon.

He was lonely.

"I wish Jeremy could play with me," he said.

Charlie watched a fuzzy worm
crawling on the sidewalk.

Charlie went inside to see Jeremy.

At story time Charlie let Jeremy
choose the story.

He taught Jeremy a new fingerplay.

He let Jeremy play with his mini cars.

When Daddy came home,

Mother asked him to go to the store.

Charlie whispered in Daddy's ear.

Daddy said out loud, "I need a helper.

Charlie, will you come with me?"

"Sure, Daddy," said Charlie.

Then Charlie went to get his bank.

He put the money in his pocket.

Charlie smiled as he thought

about the new mini car.

Daddy and Charlie bought

medicine for Jeremy.

Then they went to look at the mini cars.

Charlie picked up a shiny red one.

He had just enough money.

At home Charlie went to his room.

"Did you buy a new mini car?"

asked Jeremy.

"Yes," said Charlie, "but not for me.

I bought *you* a mini car."

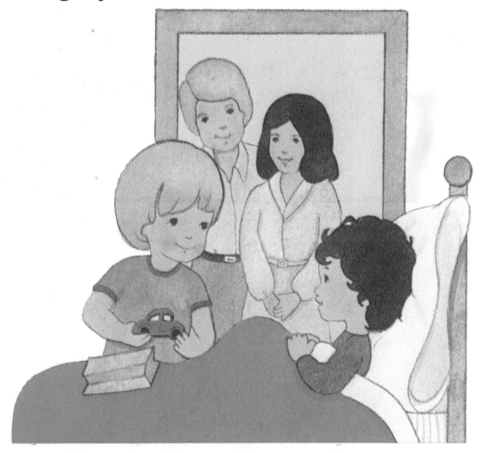

Charlie's "Be Kind" day had been very good.